# The Lupine Walker
### a journey

(27)

Forget-me-not

# The Lupine Walker
### a journey

Tony Rasch

*[signature: Tony J. Rasch]*

White Pine Publishing
Bozeman, Montana

Library of Congress Catalog Card Number: 92-80800

ISBN: 1-56044-144-5

Printed in Hong Kong

Published by White Pine Publishing, Box 6457,
Bozeman, Montana 59771,
in cooperation with SkyHouse Publishers,
an imprint of Falcon Press Publishing Co., Inc., Helena, Montana

Design, typesetting, and other prepress work by
Falcon Graphics, Helena, Montana

Caligraphy by Ann Marie Packer

Distributed by Falcon Press Publishing Co., Inc.,
P.O. Box 1718, Helena, Montana 59624, or call 1-800-582-2665

Dedicated to:   Heather Kulshan,
                my daughter,
                my gift from the mountain

# Preface

*Haiban* is a Japanese form of literature for which there is no English word. It is a travelogue that uses prose, haiku, and sometimes paintings to capture the essence of a journey.

In *The Lupine Walker*, I have attempted to write a haiban in English. Liberties have been taken that would not be allowed in Japanese: photos rather than paintings, traditional poetry as well as haiku, and a liberal interpretation regarding the form of English haiku. Nonetheless, I hope that *The Lupine Walker* does in fact capture the essence of a trip that began in Utah and ended in Canada—approximately 1,200 miles walking alone through the deserts and mountains of Wyoming and Montana.

I was 36 at the time, married, owner of a house, father of a four-year-old daughter. I had a good job where I was my own boss. I was successful by most peoples' standards. Yet I realized that I had only one life to live, and that to continue at a 40 hour week would be to die.

So, let the journey begin.

# TIME

In the beginning
God created time.
Part of it anyway.
The year, the month, the day.
The earth around the sun.
The moon around the earth.
The earth around the earth.
Who created the rest of it?
Was it the devil?
The week, the hour, the minute.
The week around the man.
The hour around his neck.
The minute around his soul.

Monday morning blues.
Alarm clocks, time clocks,
Electric clocks, wind-up clocks,
Grandfather clocks, tower clocks,
Church clocks, digital clocks,
Stop clocks.
Stop clocks?
Stop clocks!
Let go the man.
Let loose his neck.
Let free my soul!
J. G. I. F.
It's time to leave time behind.

Goodbye clocks.
I'm going to find me a river.
Follow it to its source...

I find me a river. A river in Utah called the Green. I camp on a side stream. Across the water, cliffs rise sharply and ponderosa pines catch pieces of cloud. Sitting in a reflective mood, I dedicate my journal to Heather Kulshan, my gift from the mountain, whose name she bears.

I write, "Why am I dedicating this to you, Heather, old girl? I guess because someday I think you'll want to know about your old man. I want to know about him too. Maybe on this trip, I'll find out."

Wyoming springtime
and clouds even higher
than my memory

A little cemetery lies along the road where
it crests and passes through Minnie's Gap. Jerad
Williams will lie there someday beside his brother.
He is alive when I walk through. Living on the
ranch that Minnie homesteaded. A note from his
sister will say that he died gracefully, in the spring,
while pruning his apple trees.

I spend a night behind Jerad's
orchard. Looking at a star-filled sky.
Listening to the lowing of cows.

In the desert I write, "This evening has made the walk so far worthwhile. Hot meatball stew from a sagebrush fire. How could anything taste so good...?" The still-high sun sends shafts of gold fanning out over sagebrush hills. The wind blows stiffly and leaves an occasional drop of rain.

The moon dims
scarlet gilia stars await
the rising sun


Dusty ravine:
beside a trickle of stream
buttercups in bloom

Antelope, always antelope. Usually
on the horizon. Sometimes nearby.
Always graceful. Always free.

Antelope buck
a furtive look
and then tracks

And flowers. So many. Always different.
Orange, pink, blue. Yellow, white, red.
Once a field of purple. Thousands of tiny
blooms rippling in the wind. The sky,
the clouds overhead. For a magic moment,
I am the sky, I am the clouds, I am
the wind.

Another time:

Evening primrose
four pink petals catch the sun
and quiver

One evening I enjoy the embers of a juniper fire. And the stars. One by one, they poke out. I don't know their names yet. Or their movements. That will come. The moon too. I want to learn about the moon. Probably I've read somewhere what time a full moon rises. Maybe I've even read when to expect the moon to rise ~ the next night.

Maybe.

By day, I walk. Along the Oregon Trail. Hawks overhead. Circling. Two of them playing. High in the air they circle and come together, circle and come together again. Lovers no doubt. Laughing and playing. Celebrating life.

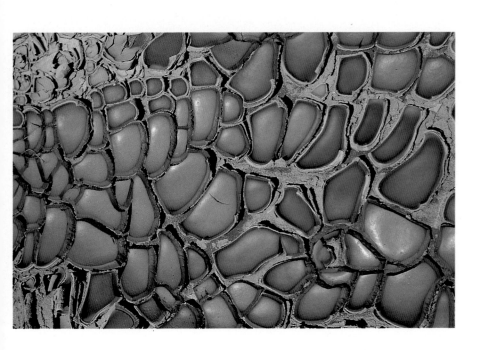

The Oregon Trail is lonely.
Full of sage and horny toads.

Hey, little horny toad
grey against grey earth
you look terrified

Morning:     From a brightening sky
             the last star fades
             a coyote howls

Then the mountains. Slowly, very slowly
the white becomes taller. The grass greener.
Desert turns to meadow. The power of the
mountains grows.

Evening:     Cloud watching evening
             the sun creeps northward
             spreading gold

Night:     All alone
           listening to frog voices
           one voice per star

Aspen trees grow at the base of the mountains. Aspen trees can dance. For joy. For life. Each leaf quivering. Full of sun. Translucent with the special green of spring.

And the song! Oh the song! A song composed of wind and sun. Rustle, rustle, rustle. I fall under their spell. I lie on my back and watch the sky dancing overhead. Flecks of sun hit the white bark. The flecks jump and leap in tune with my heart.

As the trail climbs, aspen turn to pine.

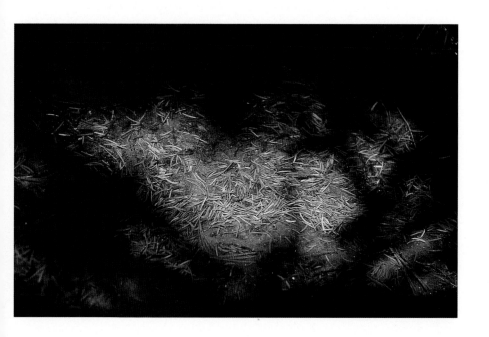

Up high the snow is vast. The wind is cold. The sky, a mixture of blue and cloud. A kaleidoscope constantly changing. Clouds come and change, come and change. From behind black towers they come and come and come. A single bee is out. It lights on a marsh marigold next to the snow.

On the summer solstice, I see a bird.

Hey, little bird,
you're walking on summer snow
aren't your feet cold?

I love the snow. Enjoy hearing it crunch underfoot. Marvel as it melts from snow to life. During the day the world becomes alive with water. Just-melted snow rushes madly downward. At night the world freezes. Water turns to ice. Flowers await the sun.

It is not easy to walk. There are no tracks.
The trail is usually covered with snow. Sometimes
cairns show the way.


Cloud-covered cairn:
briefly it seems one stone higher
Whoops! It flew away . . .

At the source of the Green River, I drink
deeply. The water is cold ~ pure ~ icy !

Old tin cup,
two holes where the handle was
water still tastes good !

From the source, the trail falls quickly.
It falls from a harsh alpine world to a warm
meadow country. Tiny alpine flowers become
large red paintbrush. White pine turns to aspen.
Columbines, wild geraniums, wild roses scent the
air. Flax and harebells add a touch of blue.

One night by Green River Lake, clouds clear. Stars come out. In the morning, Squaretop stands free, mirrored in the glassy lake. Sun caresses the mountain and creeps gently down the face.

From Piñon Ridge, I view the Tetons.
A golden ray of sun sketches a line over the
Grand. As the sun creeps northward, shadows
become very long. Greens become soft. Aspen
trunks become very white. Then just before
sunset, the world turns red. Grass, trees, and
sky burn with a soft fire. A mamma and baby
moose walk slowly by, and I laugh.

Baby moose
what a gangly creature
all humps and legs

It is the Fourth of July. The floor of
Jackson Hole is bursting with flowers.

Shadows of grass
and shadows of flowers
dance entangled

The pass into Alaska Basin is above timberline.
It has just recently become free of snow and is
alive with alpine flowers. They grow on wind-
swept ridges. Nestled down next to the ground.
Hiding in the lee of small boulders. Their roots
eat slowly away at rocks, their leaves catch
dust. When they die, they will turn to humus
and provide soil for next year's mat. The mats
spread slowly. Here a blue one, there a pink. Over
there a white or yellow or purple. Sometimes a
mixture.

Pikas, too, live up high.

Crazy coney,
your nose is twitching
don't drop the grass!

From a high Teton camp:

Hawks ~
dots against a crimson sky
will they catch the moon?

On the summit of the South Teton, all is quiet. It is a time for thinking. For munching on a Kendall Mint Bar. For feeling very small. Very happy. For merging into the universe.

Peaceful summer day
in this world of lichen ~
earth is far away . . .

I feel the happiness of being crazy. Crazy enough to leave wife and family and money. Crazy enough to walk and walk and walk. To sleep on the ground. To eat cold beans from a can. To freeze to death on the top of some mountain. Crazy enough to leave time behind, to follow a river to its source. Granite and lichen. Snow and sun. My body frozen, my soul set free. Free to fly. Free to soar!

On the shores of Lake Solitude. Small twisted pines grow from granite rocks. In barely-melted meadows, avalanche lilies glow an iridescent yellow. Long red anthers angle earthward.

Cold rain dances
on this mountain tarn
suddenly ~ sun!

On Jackson Lake there is a flower-filled
meadow. Clouds roll in from behind Moran. An
occasional flash of lightning and peal of thunder
fill the air. Then a huge black cloud opens to
reveal a patch of blue. Shafts of light descend
earthward. I watch, spellbound, as the whole
sky turns blue and the sun comes out. Karoo!
It is time for a swim!

In Yellowstone, I think of a fine
blessing for someone beginning a long trip :
"May your path be lined with lupine."

Lupine leaf shade,
just enough for my hand
and a blue butterfly

Yellowstone is mysterious. Mystery rises from the earth in clouds of steam. Even the animals feel the mystery.

Frozen fawn,
are you watching me
or the misty lake ?

The season advances.

Sweet taste of summer
ten minutes for a mouthful
wild red strawberries

An old bull moose
galumphs across the meadow
slow down heart!

My spirit dances and laughs with joy.
Paintbrush, arnica, lupine, harebells, monkshood,
buckwheat, elephant heads, gentians. Do the
names mean anything? Have you ever lain
in a field of these magic blooms?

Buttercup afternoon,
from dragonfly ripples
cloud images waver

Yellowstone. A land of flowers. A land of mist. Animals. Rivers. Lakes.

Looking north, I cross the border. Write "KAROO!" on one whole page of my journal.

Hello, Montana!

Morning's first paintbrush :
suddenly bird songs are crisper,
my pack lighter

Game trails lead through the Absarokas
Often they split and disappear in all
directions.

I camp on a flowered pass below Wallace Peak. Watch a sliver of moon follow the setting sun. See puffy clouds fade from gold to gone. Then star by star, feel the darkness come.

The path from the Absarokas to Livingston is along a road. Next to the Yellowstone. I walk at night. Through shooting stars and coyote howls. The Big Dipper pinwheels around Polaris. Orion lifts a lazy leg over jagged peaks. A rooster crows.

Montana is dry. Grass is brown.
Some flowers have already set seed. It is
a world of insects.

Grasshopper heralds
announce the coming
of a man unknown

Near Fairy Lake I write in my journal, "There is a period of a few hours in the morning when I feel like I can walk forever. The sun is up but still cool, my pack feels light, the route is along an open ridge with views in all directions and flowers at my feet. Hawks are hunting breakfast, an occasional deer goes running through white pine woods. Miles melt away as I'm carried along by a strong steady pace."

The world is full of special moments:

Slow down feet
a path of blue butterflies
is no place to hurry

Orion's not up yet,
why do you drink now,
ghostly deer?

Ah come on, elk,
the August moon is full
can't you watch quietly?

Silly fish,
you've wrinkled the moon
did it taste good?

The world is lazy.

Vast.

Ponderosa music
shall I stay for another song?
Watch a cloud move on?

Beyond the cairn,
ridge after ridge after ridge
stretches towards tomorrow...

Wild raspberry day
cup full of sweetness
ears full of conies

One evening in the Scapegoat Wilderness,
I watch a caterpillar bumping across a boulder.
I think of a caterpillar called Me. The caterpillar
called Me feels strong ~ muscles hardened by a
summer's walk, mind plucked clean, senses washed
and open. The caterpillar called Me dances and
plays and sings songs ~ with sun and wind and
magic deer. The caterpillar becomes an ouzel and
a hawk, an elk and a coney, even a mountain
for a moment or two, then a rock in a pool,
a butterfly ~ a man.

In Northern Montana, I gain a rhythm:
Waking before the sun, eating granola and berries
in a cocoon of down, striding along through long
shafts of sun. Eating, resting, thinking. Wandering.
Wandering and wondering. Reading and writing.
Watching an evening of sunset and stars. And then
waking before the sun....

Bob Marshall Wilderness :

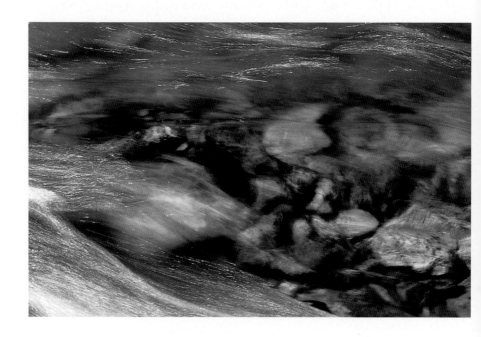

Clear sky, wet world, dew on every leaf. Clouds nestle in valleys and ravines. The Sun River reflects the sun in the sky. It floats by transparently. "Is it real?", I ask. From my old tin cup, I drink deeply and taste the answer.

Below Prairie Reef, each lupine plant
holds a silver pearl, caught at the base of seven
leaves. A female ptarmigan clucks and strolls
slowly down the trail. Leaves and stones
transform from brown to chicks ~ two and
then six. Then the six become elk ~ ten cows
and calves grazing. Gentle rays of sun illume
a deer.

Progress is slow through berry country.
I work up to a nice brisk pace and then, ohhh....
Huckleberries. Sweet, succulent, juicy. Gleaming
in the sun, swaying in the wind. Black, purple,
blue. Just one more mouthful....

The moon cycles. Days shorten. Montana
turns to fall.

Blue on the ground,
jewels on your leaves
goodbye, lupine

Ah! Sunny September,
next to buttercups still in bloom
freshly fallen snow!

Aspen alchemy :
wind and sun
into gold

Glacier Park basks in Indian summer.
The light so bright and soft it is almost tangible.
Caressing everything it touches, even the wind.
Aspen leaves rustle. A falcon circles, sending a
strange piercing call through my heart.

Above Old Man Lake, peaks of the Continental Divide touch the sky. As morning breaks, the moon sets. Patches of sun creep slowly downward. The wind is steady. The lake choppy. Waves reflect the red of mountains above. A lone teal swims toward a summit.

From Triple Divide Peak, a snow flake can melt into the Pacific, the Gulf of Mexico, or Hudson Bay. Mountain sheep straddle a ridge between north and south. Eating and dozing. An old ram watches for danger.

Later, I doze. At Red Eagle Lake, lulled to sleep by lapping waves. Eleven star-studded peaks become guardians of the night.

"For everything there is a time...." The sun lowers behind the Livingston Range. Seeds sway. Seeds, grass, rocks, myself become unified by the color red. The wind blows softly. Jupiter comes out, then stars. One by one they pop out of the fading sky.

The moon, a day past full, is slow climbing above a ridge. I awake often to watch Jupiter and the moon follow the sun's path across the heavens. Near morning, Orion is up. The Hunter is much higher than the month before.

Strawberries for breakfast, the color of snow.

Near the Canadian border, sleep is fitful. When Orion rises, I follow. Soft moon shadows fall across long white rocks. The shadows seem strange until I understand. Then I laugh at the moonstruck plants, and realize that my path is lined with lupine.

I howl at the moon and then stop and eat the last of my wild red strawberries.

# TIME

I found me a river
Followed it to its source

North into summer
Tetons and fields blazing with flowers
Stars so bright  I picked a few
Pleiades, Orion, Polaris
Strawberries in Yellowstone
Huckleberries in Glacier

The moon full and then small
Then gone and then back again
Grass turned from green to brown
Leaves to red
Frost in the morning
And days not quite so long
As the day before

I found me a river
Followed it to its source
And then a little further...

# Credits

All of the calligraphy was done by Ann Marie Packer of Olympia, Washington, who was so meticulous that sometimes she'd do a page several times to get it perfect. I am very grateful to her.

The majority of the photographs were taken by myself during moments when my pack was on the ground. The remainder were chosen to represent sights that I saw personally, but didn't get good photos of. Descriptions and credits are ordered as they appear in the book.

**Sheep Wagon** near Farson, Wyoming. TJR.

**Jerad Williams** at his home north of Dutch John, Utah. TJR.

**Strawberry cactus flowers** near Dutch John, Utah. TJR.

**Rain clouds** over the desert east of Flaming Gorge Resevoir. TJR.

**Butte** in the Flaming Gorge Natl. Rec. area. TJR.

**Field of purple flowers** south of Green River, Wyoming. TJR.

**Evening primrose** north of Green River, Wyoming. TJR.

**Drying mud** along the Green River. TJR.

**Remnants of the Oregon Trail** south of Farson, Wyoming. TJR.

**Aspen with spring leaves**, as seen along the Big Sandy River. Michael S. Sample.

**Dead pine needles in a pool** east of Big Sandy opening in the southern Wind Rivers. TJR.

**Tent door**, looking out at Cirque of the Towers. TJR.

**Pasque flowers**, southern Wind Rivers. TJR.

**Frozen marsh marigold**, central Wind Rivers. TJR.

**An alpine lake**, central Wind Rivers. TJR.

**Columbine**, northern Wind Rivers. TJR.

**Squaretop Mountain**, northern Wind Rivers. TJR.

**Sunset**, looking west toward the Tetons from the Gros Ventres. TJR

**The Tetons** from near Kelly, Wyoming. TJR.

**Alpine forget-me-nots** in Alaska Basin of the Tetons. TJR.

**Pika,** as commonly seen in the Tetons. Stan Osolinski.

**Glacier lily** near Lake Solitude in the Tetons. TJR.

**Parry's primrose** in Leigh Canyon of the Tetons. TJR.

**Tetons and Jackson Lake** from north of Colter Bay. TJR.

**Field of lupine,** as commonly seen in Yellowstone. Michael S. Sample.

**Wild strawberries** picked in northern Yellowstone. TJR.

**Bull moose,** Yellowstone. Stan Osolinski.

**Pelican,** as commonly seen on Yellowstone Lake. Michael S. Sample.

**Fringed gentian** near Yellowstone Lake. TJR.

**Red paintbrush** in the Absaroka Range of Montana. TJR.

**Frog,** as seen in willow bogs of the Absarokas. Harry Engles.

**Abandoned farm equipment** north of Livingston, Montana. TJR.

**Monkey flower blossoms** floating on stream. TJR.

**Inside of abandoned house** north of Livingston, Montana. TJR.

**Ponderosa pine,** as seen in country near York, Montana. Stan Osolinksi

**Scapegoat Wilderness,** looking northwest. TJR.

**Sun River** in the Bob Marshall Wilderness. Michael S. Sample.

**Clouds over Chinese Wall,** Bob Marshall Wilderness. TJR.

**Huckleberries,** as commonly seen in Bob Marshall Wilderness.
   Mike Javorka.

**Autumn aspen,** as seen in Glacier National Park. Stan Osolinski.

**Glacier Park alpenglow** from near Logan Pass. Stan Osolinkski.

**Moon over Glacier Park.** Stan Osolinkski.

**Heather Kulshan Rasch,** shortly after fourth birthday. TJR.

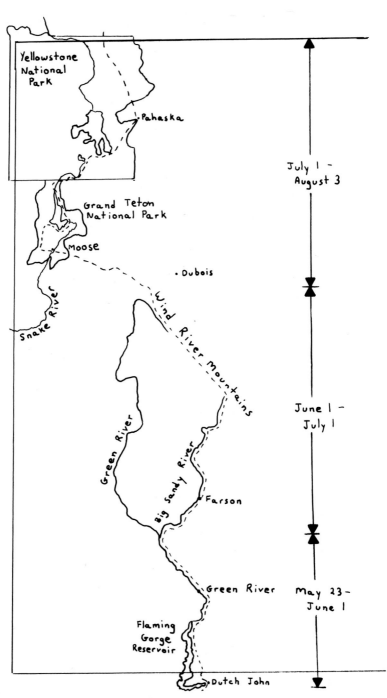

Yellowstone
National
Park

Pahaska

July 1 –
August 3

Grand Teton
National Park

Moose

Dubois

Snake River

Wind River Mountains

June 1 –
July 1

Green River

Big Sandy River

Farson

Green River

May 23 –
June 1

Flaming
Gorge
Reservoir

Dutch John

--- Approximate Route Across Wyoming

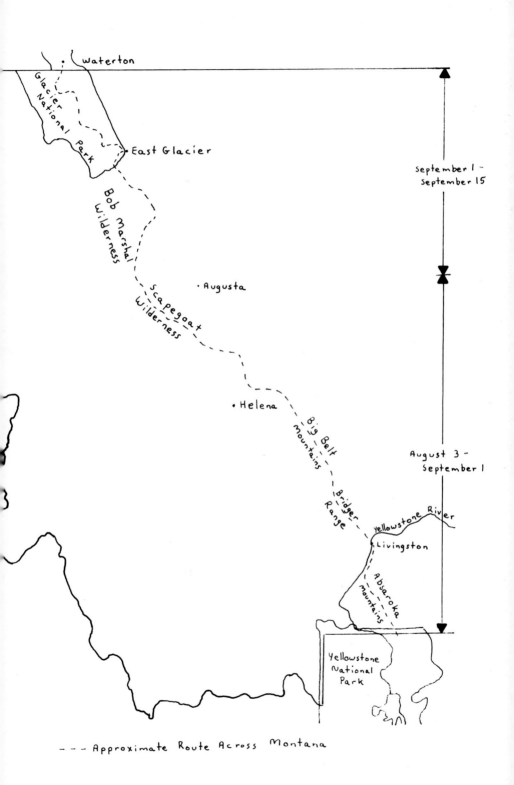

--- Approximate Route Across Montana